UP UNTIL NOW

Molly Aitken Sheridan

BookLeaf Publishing

India | USA | UK

Up Until Now© 2021 Molly Aitken Sheridan

All rights reserved.

No part of this publication may be reproduced, stored in a retrieval system, or transmitted, in any form or by any means, electronic, mechanical, photocopying, recording or otherwise, without the prior written permission of the presenters.

Molly Aitken Sheridan asserts the moral right to be identified as author of this work.

Presentation by BookLeaf Publishing

Web: www.bookleafpub.com

E-mail: info@bookleafpub.com

ISBN: 9789358361223

First edition 2021

To those in my life,

those no longer in it,

those yet to enter it -

Thank you!

ACKNOWLEDGEMENT

For those who gave me the space to write these poems, I deeply appreciate it!

For those who had no idea I was writing these poems, surprise! It's another one of my side projects you'll be reacting to with a 'You've done what now?!' look.

Thank you all for supporting me, through everything.

100% of royalties earned from this book will be split between North Edinburgh Dementia Care and the Scottish Association for Mental Health (SAMH).

PREFACE

After what seemed to be an end of the world kind of year, I wanted to express myself in a different way and take up the challenge of putting my thoughts, feelings and stories into words; crafting them into something that could live longer than scribbles on a post-it and not just living in the Notes app on my phone.

From colourful inspirations to hard to comprehend moments in my life, these poems are a little memento of what has happened up until now. I hope you enjoy reading them as much as I have enjoyed taking on this challenge to better express myself. I hope I can continue to do so.

1.

The girl with the red stick on her lips

She does it for herself

To help her smile on through

And to earn punters tips

The girl with the orange office chair,

With size that's just right

To brighten days throughout

Working at home days a 'mare

The girl with the yellow purse,

Multiple points cards she showed

He laughed with her contently

While beers and secrets flowed

The girl with the green fishtail dress

The one to show them all

Dark horse she emerged

To cut though predictable mess

The girl with the blue dressing gown

With stars and moons embossed

Its comfort brings joy

And reminders of good days past

The girl with the purple car

Seen in places she shouldn't be

Small enough for what she needs

To go places, there and also far

The girl with the pink face mask

Princess Jasmine he called her

Am I protecting myself?

The question she didn't dare ask

2.

4

Goosebumped skin being

Comforted by dawn heat as

Contemplation starts

Low breeze through long hair

Looking out into distance

White villas ahead

Happy place is here

Calm and still atmosphere helps

Settle oncoming change

3.

You can hear the voices and the laughs

The ladies catching up, awaiting

For others to arrive and watch the circle grow

Until our crew is complete

Lines and formation, places found in the room

Music starts and heart rates rise

Trainers and floor meet 'n squeak

As we warm up with direction

Performance excitement begins to build

Routines broken down, partners paired

Exhilaration and big smiles all round

One last time, just for you!

Powerful and free we feel

Behind the curtain, eagerly awaiting

Nerves circulate and in pits

On our little Denny stage

Cheers and whistles

Electric atmosphere is what is craved

To propel us into final weeks

Before we take the stage again

Surrounded by talent from all over

In awe of fellow contenders

Through screams of support

The MC exclaims YOUR MUSIC IS…ON!

A feeling like no other

Performing as one

We are a team

The passion is raw and it is real

Interminable wait until they decide

Who has come out on top

Waiting to hear the names

In first place is....

September comes and here we return

Reminiscent laughs and proud words

Of the group that we are:

Missdemeanaz, UDO World Champions!

4.

8

Jessica

Caring, Funny, Guarding, Independent, Loving

Teacher of life skills, dearly missed

Grandmother

5.

Reading the letter, the world is upside down again

Eaten away by a million emotions

Dismissal on the cards, but decision clearly made

Underestimating was the mistake however

Nicole's expertise aided my defence

Did you expect that response?

Appreciated support you eventually gave nonetheless

Now that I am in a better place

Conceal the real reasons you may but don't

You know, I rose above hurt delivered

6.

Where would I be without a sister?

Jo and I found an elixir

The laughs, fights and the rest

We put bond to the test

Be nowhere without my sister

7.

The power of expression is true

Beat in my heart, impressing you

Wearing things that no-one else does

Born to stand out, that's us

Unique, don't forget

Remember me

As we met

As I

Do

8.

You are the reason I write this

Helping hands that have guided me through

Cannot thank you enough for all you have done

When the pressure was on and pain had only just begun

Love and support was right there on cue

Untruths and self-deprecation you were quick to dismiss

Giving me time of day when it's time to reminisce

To go over the things I thought I knew

Cannot thank you enough for all you have done

You knew that I was nowhere near the end of my run

And everything was solved with a brew

You are the reason I write this

Warding off evils deserving of resist

Bringing me up as returning confidence grew

Cannot thank you enough for all you have done

To those who brought my vision back into clear view

You are the reason I write this

Cannot thank you enough for all you have done

9.

This place is now my home

The next stop on the tour

Of finding out who I am

I'm on this journey alone

This place is actually quite small

Will everything fit in?

This hand-me-down table's too big

Not too sure 'bout this at all...

This place is cold

Air vent, what the hell?!

Heating spreads only one way

Jumper wearing has increased two fold

This place is dated

Pay as you go electric meter?

And what are these strange marks?

Maybe I should have waited...

This place is actually not that bad

There's a spot for all my hoardings

And there's even room for a desk

Maybe I won't become a nomad

This place is starting to take shape

Connections with giveaways galore

Loved ones round to make it more homely

Sticking down the rug with tape

This place is now safe

Everything is in situ and will stay

And visitors have approved

No longer feeling like a waif

This place is now my own

The space to allow me to recover

And new experiences to uncover

I realise now I am not alone

As this place is now my home

There once was a girl who laughed a lot

Her smile would lead with a giggle at God knows what

Her outlook is sunny

When everything is funny

Her positivity was something well sought

11.

Warm smile,

That could turn any frown upside down.

Cautiously wondering,

Should, would, could.

Endless yearning,

For what was, more of what is, the wonder of what if.

Protective hand,

Held through the hardest of times.

Calming voice,

Over breathless tears down the phone.

Supportive notwithstanding,

Who you really are and have become.

Longing stares,

That have words due to be shared.

Seeing them again,

Running and jumping into their arms.

Hearts racing,

Filled with affection and joy.

Blinding love,

Cannot see the truth through it.

Little moments,

That are forgotten but not lost.

The little bird, trapped in a cage

Looking out into the big world, out there

Felt like this from such a young age

It wants its chance to take centre stage

But through the bars, the others said 'Beware!'

The little bird, trapped in a cage

It wants its freedom to engage

But the high walls add to this nightmare

Felt like this from such a young age

Shocked looks if it shows any rage

Who can answer a simple prayer?

The little bird, trapped in a cage

It doesn't want to upstage

It just wants to show why they are so rare

Felt like this from such a young age

Opening that door will certainly assuage

And welcome in fresh freedom air

The little bird, trapped in a cage

Felt like this from such a young age

Do not wake me

For I am tired

Of all the things

That have fallen through

Those dreams I had

Have not come true

Plans that were made Have now fallen through

What for it now?

What do I do?

It feels as though

This life's fallen through

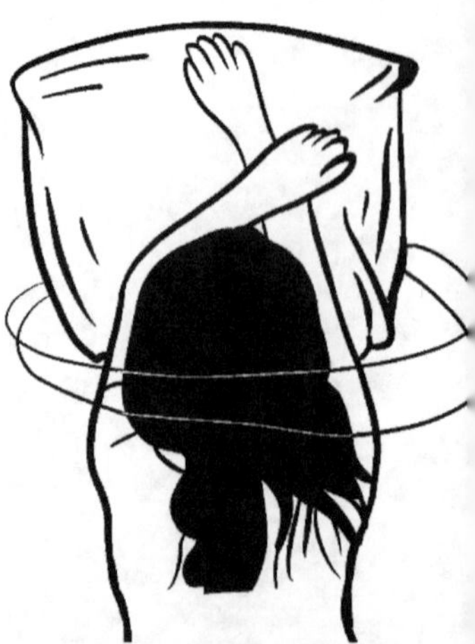

The day isn't over

Not everything is blue

Only one who can

Change it is you

14.

The one that has been hiding in plain sight

Something has always been there

A concealed spark yet to ignite

And now we are here, no time to spare

The long-awaited meet to convey

Those hidden feelings, reminiscing on the past

Subsequent embraces in doorways, repressed emotions on display

We pull in closer, protection from pounding rain

And now there is little to discuss

We have completed our amends

The best scenario for both of us

Return to our roots, as friends

Until we meet once more…

Our cheeks will be blushed

By our encounters before

Do you ever wish time would just stop?

So you can stay in a moment,

For as long as possible

And not face what's coming.

Safe in this comfort

And protected

From all that's

Ahead of

You.

16.

In this dark room I fear

As I long into nothing

What are they thinking of me?

I cannot ask, they are nowhere near

The long journey round my thoughts

Spiralling in and out of the past

The anxiety ripples through

Overwhelming and so vast

What is the root of this?

A moment of recklessness

Or an embedded habit?

Endless cycle of doubt

Is this the end?

Of what I thought I knew

What is the plan now?

Do I have the energy to defend?

Will they still be there for me?

Now I have revealed another side

That hasn't seen the light of day before

The side that has been told to abide

Then the moment comes

A sign of life appears

That pulls me from dormant state

To face everything now on my plate

17.

Here we are again

Facing truths that have been freed

Shame, disgust and tears

I've destroyed what we have built

Hurt caused, permanently here

18.

Away from gloomy Onslow conditions

And an escape from family nests

A safe little sanctuary

Located in the South West

Walking through the snow

Left by the Beast from the East

The city was pretty much closed

But Iceland at the Cross was open at least

Being awakened to a recap

Of a fun-filled night

Loved hearing the drunk antics

It must have been some sight

Late night loops on YouTube

From RuPaul to favourite Vines thereafter

Singing along to Ayo Technology

I can still hear our fits of laughter

Loud bangs in the close outside

Neighbour shouting through angry tears

Breaking off door handles in rage

'You were only going out for '4 or 5 beers!!''

Pulling the curtains off the railings

From just falling off my bed

A freak moment messing around

Now crippled me with awful dread

Last minute reference writing

Sponsored by that fourth cup of coffee

Was finally replaced

By a bag from the offy

Recorded moments of stupidity

'I'm from Leeds' & 'Oh Hello There'

There's plenty of wild outtakes

One's not to share!

All the birthdays, quiz nights and get-togethers

We really made the place our own

Plenty of memories were made

We were definitely not alone

It was a place to bond

And a place to be free

With my two favourite people

Who experienced it with me

19.

Unwritten or in place

Unspoken or said

They are meant to be broken

The rules that we were born to defy

Running wild and untamed

Consequences become irrelevant

Finding out who we are

Experimenting with everything in our way

Fleeing those who instruct the law

Across fields of dreams

Change will soon knock upon the door

Thank goodness for rebellion

Living outrageously as possible

Before it takes it all back

Taking the stand

And sticking it to 'The Man'

Because why not?

Can't knock it until you try it, eh?

There is something bigger out there

It won't wait up for those in stationary view

'What if?' seems to be the hardest thought

Missed opportunities will wave you goodbye

Many routes and directions unexplored

Unless seekers take the plunge

Comfort will only go so far

Indulge in the dangerous

One chance and one time offers

Will become few and far between

38

Don't ignore that urge

That feeling, that itch

The calling is here

And it is time to go

20.

Hands on shoulders retreating

Perceptions and known behaviours

Have tied down, locked away

Multiple emotions that have been competing

To be the one victorious, saviours

In their own right, but hard to convey

Up until now

This open space and time, abounding

Unseen paths ahead

Expectations to oppose

New found freedom, now grounding

Intoxicating feeling now wide spread

Never existed, never disclosed

Up until now

Lessons learned, to be applied

Marks and scars within, to be healed

The story continues to be penned

Opinions and judgements collide

A new position to yield

Difficult pit to now ascend

Up until now

Rush of joy floods over

No retreats to previous positions

Afresh fire burns through unnecessities and

Unsolicited invitations to return

To unforgiving conditions

That were once high in demand

Up until now

The clarity of the light unfolds

Reflections of the past

Present but not in control

Ever growing character to remould

New journeys to begin at last

And stories unknown to the soul

Up until now

9 789358 361223